Dear Indie Author

Dear Indie Author

Tonya Nagle PhD

N^2

N^2: Nagle-North Publishing
2020

Dear Indie Author

Dear Indie Author

By Tonya Nagle, PhD

1. Creative Writing 2. Creative Business 3. Author Planning

Cover design by Tonya Nagle

Printed in the United States of America

Creative Writing With Dr. Nagle www.creativewritingwithdrnagle.com

ISBN:

N2: Nagle-North Publishing
North Carolina

www.creativewritingwithdrnagle.com

Dedication

To writers everywhere, foolow your heart and write your story!

Contents

Cara North

I can't start this book without explaining a few things. Yes, I am an indie author and I have been for a very long time. Why haven't you heard of me before? Well, you may not have heard of Cara North either, but chances are greater you will have come across her books rather than my academic writing as Tonya Nagle. Cara North is my pseudonym. Cali Kent is another one, but I only have one title out under that name. I wish I would have just put it under Cara all those years ago, but back then, I was following every direction but my own.

This book is not set up to tell you what to do, rather I am telling you my story and giving you knowledge so you can choose your own adventure with a bit more clarity than I was offered. Please, don't get me wrong, I have an entire shelf of books about writing published by several major publishers and several are written by household names. I did learn from those books. Unfortunately, those books were set up for authors with a traditional publishing path. I've rarely done anything the traditional way.

Making my own path is sort of my trademark trait. I find a way. That is just what I do. What I have realized from years of motivating other writers is that I am good at this task. I have a lot of information and a different perspective from what is out there in most threads. Therefore, I also have a responsibility to share that knowledge and hopefully, make some other writer's life and journey a more informed one if not easier.

This is it. This is my debut creative writing project as Tonya Nagle and it is filled with information I think you could find useful if you are about to, or if you have already, set out on this endeavor.

If you would like to participate in other ways you can find more information on the website: www.creativewritingwithdrnagle.com and you can find the podcast on most listening outlets by the same name.

End of the Contract

This essay will be short and to the point, like your writing career if you don't pay attention to it. When you get a contract for your work it is often so exciting for you, your family, and friends. Even if you get a legal person to look at it, they are generally focused on the positives, the beginning. What you really need to look out for is the end. I'm not a lawyer and this is not legal advice. Hopefully, reading this will ensure you read your contracts completely and if you need to see a lawyer, that will be obvious to you sooner.

In this day of technology and electronic publication of work more prevalent than ever, you MUST look at the end of contract terms and you have to push yourself to the end, to that scenario and a few others, before signing anything.

What I am about to share are my personal experiences. I am making them as general as possible so as not to tarnish the reputation of others, but if you have been in the industry a while you probably know someone who has experienced the same or a similar situation. If you are new, then this is for you. I'm only airing some dirty laundry here so that you may be able to keep from falling into the same puddles of mud.

Small press publishers were opening and closing so frequently in the 90s that it was difficult to feel comfortable anywhere. There were two kinds of publishers at this point, ones who closed and gave you all of your money and your rights back, and the ones who closed and didn't pay you, give your rights back, or give you any indication as to what was going to happen to your work and in what timeframe.

Most of us that survived those times learned not to sign a contract unless it had a clause in it for what happened if THEY were not successful. Most contracts up to that point had been about what happened if YOU, the AUTHOR, was not performing according to the publisher's standards. In the wake of those publishers (when I say small press, I don't mean small dollars) closing, thousands of authors found themselves not sure what was happening to their money, but more importantly, their book rights.

Why are the book rights more important? Because rights are the future of that author's money. If the stories were kept as part of bankruptcy the author now has no right to the book that with a closed publisher is no longer published. It is essentially a dead document. The other scenario is a closing that may not have been bankrupt, but poor management of closing documentation by the publisher resulted in no point of contact to get rights released back to the author in writing. This means that the author cannot prove to any other publisher, or if self-publishing, to those distribution outlets that the rights have been reverted. Fortunately, I was able to get release of rights from my publishers before they closed.

It's not just small press publishers though. Distribution outlets can also fall apart or change. One such distributor had to close and issued a payment option of a fraction of what was owed or if the people wanted all the money then it would be settled in court. Unfortunately, that distributor also allowed for publication of work under their banner as the publisher, so some authors had to engage in the battle over money and publishing rights. It isn't just independent programs though. There is no secret that Kindle Worlds were dissolved, and while Amazon was the publishing platform and handled some of the situation, the rights to those KW stories belonged in part to the author of the world you wrote in, because in order to publish in their world, you had to include elements, characters, or some detail of that nature. Therefore, Amazon was not responsible for the fallout of the dissolved worlds.

I wrote in a few of these worlds and I was blessed that the owners of those worlds essentially asked us to remove the connections and we could re-publish our books. I revised my books and placed two of them back up for sale and now use the other two as promotional material. Some authors were even kind enough to say-just publish it as is but add specific information so readers would also connect back to them. I had that option but chose to break from their world completely.

Others have taken the system and launched their own "world based" publishing platform. This is where the main author created a publishing house so they were still able to control the world, authors could still be invited to write in it, and they could still publish that work unaltered.

All the above were, in my professional opinion, honorable options. Still, there were horror stories of world owners that decided not to give any direction for what could or could not be used, how to change or modify, etc. I don't hear about the complications of this situation often anymore, so I imagine it has gone the way of small press, distribution, and branches of a New York houses that closes without warning meaning only those still entangled in the turmoil feel the pain. Fortunately, I am not one of those people.

I didn't care much about the beginning or end of the "world" contracts. At this stage of my writing career, I should have known better. Things worked out for me and I wrote in the worlds of some amazingly kind and candid authors, so I didn't have a lot of stress other than the task of revising those books. I say that to say this, even those of us who have been writing for over a decade have to remind ourselves to begin with the end in mind. Next time you get a contract or want to participate in something, make sure you know about the contract ending. What happens if they, the publisher close? What happens if this group writing project falls apart? You may still lose money, but if you have your writing back, you can revise it or re-release it and make your own money from it. If they have the rights, you won't have money or a book.

I'm not Judy Blume

I'm sure you're thinking, "No shit!"

What I mean by this statement is that Judy Blume is the woman who wrote *Frecklejuice* and she is also the woman who wrote *Wifey*. I'm sure a lot of you are familiar with the first one, but not everyone will be familiar with the second. *Wifey* is a dirty book. Spoiler alert: it begins with a man masturbating on the main character's front lawn. I think that is the entire summary you will need to understand that not every author can be Judy Blume. We can't all write using one name. I don't. Cara North is a pseudonym created on a slow evening in the writing lab at the community college I was teaching for at the time. Several of my co-workers and I came up with it from a list of possibilities. The theory was that people would connect Cara North to North Carolina, where I began my publishing career and where I currently live.

Now, I don't teach K-12 students as a profession, so I wasn't worried that they would discover me. I do teach adult learners: college students, military personnel, and some writing workshops in libraries, and at senior centers. Out of consideration for the fact that not all of them would be understanding about the fact that their teacher also wrote a lot of filthy sex scenes in fiction, I began my writing under a pen name.

I'm not the only one who does this. A lot of authors do, even if they do not write sexually explicit content. Take Eloisa James, for example. Mary Bly is a tenured Shakespeare professor. I remember listening to an Audible Original podcast titled *Authorized: Love and Romance* where she admitted that it took her several years before she let her co-workers know that she was historical romance author, Eloisa James.

Men use women's names, women use men's names, and a whole bunch of people just use initials. Why? Maybe it is to further their anonymity. Maybe, it is so as a reader, you don't attempt to put a gender on the author and make assumptions about the content due to that gender. Regardless of the why, this has been happening since the beginning of publishing.

The pros to having a pseudonym is that you have some level of anonymity. The cons to having a pseudonym is that you are essentially stuck with it once you begin using it, and there is also another person out there in the world who likely actually has that name. There may even be another author if you publish long enough. Then what? There are no copyright laws on names, so if you are thinking of using a name, take it for a spin on the internet. Eventually, you may be just as flabbergasted as I was a few years ago.

See, I occasionally take both my real name and my pseudonym for a search engine ride just to see what pops up. Usually, nothing out of the ordinary, but then it happened. It wouldn't be strange to discover these names attached to social media profiles or other careers, but I have discovered that there is a Tonya Nagle out there writing romance novels and there is a Cara North in instructional design presenting at conferences and teaching in higher education. I have contacted neither of these women but have interacted with Tonya in a Facebook thread or two since we run in some similar digital circles. It was weird to say the least! This is not to say that your career doppelganger is out there. I'm simply trying to give you a glimpse into the reasons I chose to use a pen name and then how, after fourteen plus years, it really didn't matter.

What matters is that I have two, technically three, identities today and my books are in multiple formats, so I can't just streamline them without disrupting narrators and cover artists to make those changes. It simply is not worth it for me to do that.

Think about it when you make the decision to publish. Pick a name that is going to settle into your identity for the rest of your life.

Check to see if anyone else is writing under that name (at least if it is in your genre you may want to change it to avoid confusion). Several of my friends have pseudonyms for each of their wiring personas. They use this name to write one genre, another to write in the next, and still more names if they write with partners. Maybe we should all try to be more like Judy Blume. If I had just started with my name, I wouldn't have to hold a double identity today. Still, as I contemplate expanding my writing into Young Adult and Sci-Fi/Fantasy, I am considering adding yet a fourth or fifth name to my roster. I am definitely not a Judy Blume kind of writer. I want the separation. Even if it means rethinking my entire plan.

If you would like more information on this, you can look up my Teachable class called Name Calling. It's free and won't take longer than thirty minutes to go through though it may take you days, weeks, months, or even years to decide on the perfect name for your writing persona.

Here are some of my pros and cons. The worksheet on the next page is for you to list out yours.

Pros	Cons
Anonymity_____	Another name to track__
Reader easily IDs genre	Another brand to market
Write new and start fresh	Brainstorming names__

Notes

Pros and Cons Pseudonym Worksheet

List of Pros

List of Cons

_____

_____

_____

_____

_____

_____

_____

_____

_____

_____

_____

_____

_____

_____

_____

_____

_____

_____

_____

_____

_____

_____

_____

_____

_____

_____

_____

_____

_____

_____

_____

_____

_____

_____

_____

_____

_____

_____

_____

_____

_____

_____

Notes

Possible Choices

Some examples from my own decisions for the YA and SC-Fi/Fantasy brainstorming. Keep in mind my current pseudonyms are Cara North and Cali Kent. Both are abbreviations based on states.

Pseudonym	Meaning/Reason
Dakota South___	Similar to Cara North_____
Cara South_____	As in new direction for Cara__

I have more and some are good some are terrible, but it is the process and you have to go through it if you want to make a good decision in the end.

I went with the following:

Echo North for Science Fiction and Fantasy
September North for Young Adult

Tagline: Head North for all of your reading needs.

Some people consider the target audience and the names that were established as popular during that audience's birth. You can also go with classic names that span demographics and don't go out of style.

Genre picking is another way to decide on a name. If you notice, a lot of Sci-Fi/Fantasy books have authors with initials and a last name on the cover. If you are trying to decide what are the cool names for a genre then do a search for the top selling titles in the market and see what kind of names pop up. Are they short, long, complicated or simple? It might help you fit in as you also stand out.

I know what I am about to say will sound contradictory since my Creative Writing With Dr. Nagle website is literally that name. I am writing non-fiction and it is all within the creative writing field. I'm a coach, so my name is what propels my site. However, when it comes to fiction, I have had Cara North as a website and I prefer having Sirens and Muses. Why? Because with Sirens and Muses I can write whatever genre under whatever name I want. It becomes more like my publishing platform than just my author website. That's my input for what it is worth. I'm trying not to manage a site for every single name I write under when the majority of readers will find me on social media and on book outlets not my website. Having it is important, but limiting it by one author name for fiction is not what I want to do.

You can take the letters in your legal name and jumble them around to make a new name. You can play one of those games on the internet like what would your dragon slayer name be (I don't know if that is a real game, but you get the idea) and see what comes out of it. Maybe you always wanted to be called something other than what your parents put on your certificate. Use that name.

I like to post a poll and see what other people think about what I am working on. After all, some of those people will be purchasing my work and some of those people are other writers who know what works in certain genres. There is nothing wring with crowdsourcing brainstorming. You don't have to use any of those names, but one might stick or be the suggestion that gets you to what you are looking for.

Note: Please do not choose something like C.U. Cumming unless you are writing parody or those truly are meaningful initials and you are NOT writing romance.

Notes

Pseudonym Brainstorming Worksheet

Name: _____

Meaning/Reason:

_____

_____

Name: _____

Meaning/Reason:

_____

_____

Name: _____

Meaning/Reason:

_____

_____

Name: _____

Meaning/Reason:

_____

_____

Name: _____

Meaning/Reason:

_____

_____

Sometimes it Just Sucks

Being a creative person is supposed to be fun and filled with praise and admiration. It is. Sometimes. Other times, it just sucks. I need to tell you this because if you are trying to base your success on the "wins" known as best seller status, big royalty checks, etc. then you may feel like a loser more often than not, even if you hit those benchmarks at some point.

Redefine success. Think about all the great authors, painters, musicians, and more who we celebrate and use for education purposes across the globe as examples of brilliant creators. A decent amount of them were not even acknowledged in their own time. You do not have to be a suffering artist to be an artist. You do not have to be a best seller to be meaningful or relevant. You do have to decide what success means to you and possibly re-define success several times throughout your career.

My example of this is begins in my writing for publication beginning. My goal was to be a *New York Times* (NYT) Bestselling Author. Here's the thing about being a NYT Bestselling author, very few independent titles will make it there without the backing or funding of a major publisher. Little did I know then about how much an editor at a major publishing house can change your book to make it more...saleable? I didn't know back then how much the marketing department had control over the book cover, the blurb, the entire campaign. I didn't know, until I was an author at a few small-press publishers, how much that would bother me.

Even at a small press, the publishing house has editors and they give input not just typo corrections. You can be sure in several contracts the editorial team has the right to change if the author does not come to that conclusion with a little suggesting. Authors can often fill out sheets about what they would like to see on a book cover, but you guessed it. The graphics department will ultimately decide what it will look like. After going through this process a few times with smaller presses, combined with meeting more traditionally published authors, I became less impressed and more protective of my art.

Decisions must be made in situations such as this. The right decision for me, as my contracts came to an end, was to ask for my rights back. My control back. With that came the quest for what success was going to look like if I was not going to be traditionally published anymore. I decided that having control was more important. I then decided to define success based on sales.

Success based on sales is a never-ending war where you win one battle and lose the other. My sales were pretty good at the start of my writing. I had some books in small press houses and started publishing my own as I waited for those other titles to come back to me. When I was writing and publishing about once a month, things were moving along. I was working part-time and going to college and my spouse was deployed a lot.

Then came full-time employment, my PhD coursework, moves, and non-deployment cycles for my spouse. Suddenly, I had no time for my writing, much less the upkeep of promoting it. Sales tapered off until there were months when I was lucky to get a royalty check that would cover a cup of fancy coffee much less pay a bill or for other promotion materials.

I had to reassess and re-define success.

Success became about completing work rather than how much of it sold. I am a writer. It is a part of my being. I was writing stories when I was a child and I will likely be writing them in Valhalla. I am going to write what I want to write, how I want to write it, plain and simple.

I do not need anyone's permission to do that. It was one of the takeaways I got from Gretchen Rubin's book *Big Magic*. She validated something I had believed all along. I don't have to be miserable; my art doesn't have to be built out of pain and tragedy, and I don't need anyone else to like it. I must like it. You must like what you write. It is totally okay to just have fun and enjoy the process. It is awesome to celebrate your milestones and to count getting one more thing on the list done.

I meet people all the time and they are serious writers, very serious writers. A decent amount of them are not published. Probably never will be. They should keep writing, yes. They should also stop judging me. I get a lot of judgment. If I had grown up differently, if I had not made my way by trial and fire, I would likely have quit long ago. However, I did. I won't let someone else's opinion about the genre I choose to write in or the fact that I write for entertainment rather than whatever it is they seem to believe they are writing for. If it is fiction it is still a form of entertainment. Writers can be a very judgmental group of people. My suggestion is to choose your peers wisely.

They are after all, just peers. I don't care if they won the whatever award for most awesome author on the planet. At the end of the day, the next book is waiting, the next book for that author to write and the next book the reader will pick up while waiting for an author to write. Readers may follow authors, buy the books, review them even, but it does not mean that they have one interest and one genre. It never hurts to remind yourself that this book may be the right book for millions. The next book may only connect with ten people. Okay, write the third book, and the fourth, and so on.

Will there be cliques. Of course, there will. Event staff will pick and choose who may attend. Other authors will pick and choose who they will publicly support. All of this is okay because it is their career and you don't want to be somewhere you are not wanted anyway. Right?

Do not let what other authors are doing define your success. If you can't get into an event as an author, find another venue. If that doesn't work, do some research and plan your own. What I learned from both Mindy Kaling's *Why Not Me?* and Jenna Fischer's *The Ac-*

tor's Life is that you have to take charge of your own artistic career. If it is going well or bombing, you are the only one able to grab it and change direction, push it forward, or pull it to a halt for intense evaluation. Additionally, you are the only one responsible for doing any or all the above. It is your career. Be the Chief Executive Officer (CEO) and the janitor. If you can afford a personal assistant or virtual aid, great, but if you cannot do that job in the interim if they bail, you have a problem. They may get paid for tasks, but you are the one responsible for ensuring all the work is done. All of it.

Maybe you need a break.

I needed a serious break when I was in my PhD program. There was one point where I was working full-time, my spouse was deployed, and I was losing my hair and gaining weight despite any adjustments I made to diet and exercise. I was tired, aching, and then the heart palpitations began. Needless to say, within a few weeks I was sent to an endocrinologist and diagnosed with Hashimoto's Thyroiditis, a form of hypothyroidism with the added bonus of being an autoimmune disorder. It took almost two years for them to get my levels straight.

I am eternally grateful to the endocrinology department at Bethesda! My hair stopped falling out, my weight at least stabilized, and I understood what was happening. I didn't like it, and still don't, but at least I understood.

Writing during that time was in journals and for personal reasons. I was not capable or interested in sitting down to write fiction when journal writing had always been the method I used to make sense of things and to process. Again, when you stop writing and take a hiatus, you must re-define success. During those years, I defined success as not losing every reader I had gained. It was a success to complete my homework and the research necessary to get to the next course in my program of study. I was writing, a lot, and it was meaningful…in an academic sort of way.

Watching my sales dwindle to nothing sucked. It absolutely, positively, sucked. However, I remained a published author and that is still an accomplishment. I continued to flip all the negatives into positives. Then my dissertation committee fell apart and I was without a chair. No chair, no completion. While I searched for a new chair, I enrolled in another program. A creative writing program. It revitalized me, reminded me of what I had been missing out on. The fun. My dissertation was not fun in the least. The research and essays leading up to it was not exactly a trip to a theme park either. It was quite frankly depressing. If you would like to read my dissertation and have access to scholarly databases, you can find it. I am pretty sure I am still the only Tonya Nagle, PhD in there.

The truth is if you are writing with the sole purpose of making money, you are writing for the wrong reason and it will be a painful event for as long as that remains your primary goal. If you are writing because you enjoy writing, because you have stories to tell, something important to say, an experience other people need to learn about or can relate to, then writing will be what you had hoped for: a satisfying adventure where every reader makes a difference in your life and every sale feels like the lottery. Will you make a lot of money? Maybe. Maybe not. Should that stop you from being a writer? No. If it does, then you were never really a writer, you were someone thinking writing is an easy way to make money.

Maybe you are a hobbyist or a dabbler. It is totally okay to be both. I'm a hobbyist at several things and dabble in even more. I am not dedicating a committed portion of my life and identity to those things. Speaking of identity, especially for those hobby and dabble writers, please never think you are hiding behind a pseudonym. It may give you some level of anonymity, but anyone with a computer and the desire to know who you are can figure it out. Ghost writers get found out and their whole job outside of writing the book is to remain a secret.

There are at least eighty other scenarios where this whole thing can suck. You put your heart and soul into a graphic just to hear someone say that the font is terrible. You buy ink pens with your name on them just to learn that the ink runs so no one can use them. You put your name on everything just to learn that no one wants to wear YOUR NAME on their body, so your shirts end up as lawn clothes or if you're lucky as a sleep shirt. Writing is the most fun part of this, so if you don't like the writing, you may want to step back and figure out why you are pursuing it.

Most writers I know enjoy the writing, it's the marketing that sucks the most. My personal marketing experience is strange because I can promote something else, someone else, all day long, but my own work, I get extra shy, nervous, and it has taken me YEARS to figure out that I DESERVE the payment for the work I do. I'm not churning out the same story and characters over and over. I give them all new issues and complications that I took time to research before assigning. I have read multiple manuals on sex and positions and preferences in order to bring you safe, explorative sex (yes, it is a bit exaggerated, but it's fiction). Most people do not do what I write in the books. To be honest, I DO NOT DO the things I write in these books. However, I have researched and when possible spoken to many people who DO, before I put a little more embellishment on it.

I mention this because it SUCKS when you write romance, but especially if you write erotic romance that everyone somehow thinks you do everything you write. I always counter with a comment along the lines of, "How many people have James Patterson or Stephen King actually murdered? When was the last time you saw John Grisham running from a court room because someone on the jury was going to kill him?" It is fine if people want to ask me about resources or share information (well beyond what is normally comfortable to hear while eating a meal) but to assume or imply that I must because my characters do is to hold me to another standard. I like to be held to the same standard as everyone else (by everyone else I mean men).

Maybe I am wrong. Maybe people believe that Tom Clancy is really Jack Ryan, but I somehow doubt it.

If you are a man and you are reading this, I am not trying to unsettle you, I am just trying to plant a seed of discretion and level of informed discussion when you speak to someone, anyone writing romance (because plenty of men write romance and have since books were published). Why am I calling out the men folk? Simple, in all my years of writing and publishing I have never been asked by a female if "this" (my book in hand) is what my sex life is like. In fact, the first and last time my spouse picked up one of my books to read, he skimmed through and said, "Uh, what?" I replied with, "Not for you, dude. Not happening." Then he looked at this contemporary, erotic romance writer and said, "Prude." I shrugged. That was the end of it and as close to my bedroom readers ever need to come.

What you write in fiction is NOT who you are or what you are in real life. You DO NOT need to be a woman/man/minority/majority/etc. member to write authentic characters. You DO need to research, and not just surface news kind of research. Talk to people to find out what stereotypes bother them the most. Everyone has stereotypes and you may want to use those in your work to bring light to them or ensure you avoid them so as not to perpetuate the misconception. Talk to people about real situations. I have never met anyone who didn't want to help me get something right.

Be aware that no one person represents the whole. If NFL football player Colin Kaepernick taught the world anything it is that talking to one Veteran for how to handle his political view was not representative of the entire military population's opinion. Much like that situation, there are going to be people who like it, hate it, and find common ground for it. Much like Colin, every decision you make, may someday bite you in the ass no matter how much you researched it. If people want to hate you, they will. They will find a way to be ugly even if you did not intend to upset them.

I am not going to let other people dictate what kind of characters I write. They have the option to pick up another title. I don't intentionally offend anyone, and I am aware that even with that, I might. I get offended all the time and manage to keep going. I've probably offended at least one person reading this book by now because I use curse words in it. Such is life. We don't live in a safe space. If you are reading, if you are writing, you definitely do not create in a safe space. You are just as dangerous with your words as readers are with their opinions of them. All you can do is research and then write your characters authentically as they form.

If research of that nature makes you uncomfortable then write in the sci-fi paranormal genre where you can completely make shit up, right? Only the problem is you still have to build a society and you still create multiple races and probably governments, etc. You get to change the things around and maybe create something totally fantastical, but you must be careful if you don't like to do research. I mean, think about it. If you have no desire to appreciate the wealth of diversity in your real life, you are not likely to create a wealth of diversity in your fiction which will make for a flat population and readers won't "buy it" or purchase it.

Sometimes writing sucks. Research can be fun, but it means work away from writing the story, and sometimes that really sucks. Sometimes people suck. They make assumptions about your life or what you know because of what you write. Sometimes I suck, because I am telling you things you may already know and possibly didn't want to hear, or maybe needed to know and hear but it still sucks.

Guess what, sometimes you suck. That's right, dear reader, sometimes you also suck because we (me as a reader included) do not always remember what went into creating something before offering it up for judgement in this world. Before getting published I did write reviews for a popular magazine. I can't tell you how badly I want to take one of those reviews back, but alas, I cannot. What I didn't know then, I learned after becoming an author. Now, I only leave stars and brief words if I review something at all. If I didn't like a book, I chalk it up as a lesson and determine what I didn't like about it and how I can ensure I am not making the same mistake in my writing. Even bad books can teach you something. Just like bad leaders taught me what I didn't want to become, bad books teach me what I don't want to be known for as a writer.

Also, a bad book to me may be an awesome book to someone else. You may think this is a bad book, but I think it is a valuable resource for new and emerging authors. Understanding that because it wasn't the right book for me to enjoy, but may be the book someone else loves, reminds me to stop and think. Who am I to say it is crap? I am not saying you should not give a book a bad review, even this one if you feel so strongly about it but do so with kindness and genuine comments. If you are reading this book you are probably in pursuit of publication or you are looking for new perspective as an indie author. Know that if you are a snarky, careless reviewer you will get reviewed by a snarky, careless reviewer and chances are you are not going to handle that well.

Ready for the last part that really sucks. Even if you are the most kind and generous reviewer out there, someone is going to try to throw a cloud in front of your rainbow and ruin your day because they can. What can I say? Sometimes this writing thing…sucks. I'm still going to do it anyway and so should you!

Success Worksheet

Personal Success means:

_____

_____

_____

Professional Success means:

_____

_____

_____

Biggest Fears of Failure:

_____

_____

_____

Biggest Fears of Success:

_____

_____

_____

Quotes That Motivate You:

_____

_____

_____

_____

_____

_____

Marketing is for Masochists

Okay so technically the definition of a masochist is that you are going to derive some sexual gratification from your pain, but let's get real here, in 2020 we use that term to describe anyone who seems to keep coming back for more even though whatever it is makes them miserable for a time. If you are lactose intolerant but you can't resist a scoop of ice-cream, you are going to feel a lot of discomfort if not pain later, and yet you eventually get another scoop.

Marketing is like that for me. I hate it, but I also kind of enjoy it. It makes me miserable and worried but is also fun coming up with new ideas and designs. I have this very twisted relationship with marketing and that is why the header is what it is. It is both pleasure and pain. I can confidently say that I have never had any sexual delight from my marketing, but if I hit a million sales I won't rule out a little titillation from it (Let's just be honest, if you sold a million copies your whole body is going to light up and mine would too). Every author's goal should be to run a campaign so strong and hard that it gets them to orgasm (over a million sold copies).

Alas, I am still in the trenches and telling myself it is all worth the pain and effort if I get more than 20 sales on release day. So why are you taking advice from a loser like me?

Well, part of the reason is because this loser is a much better coach than a practitioner. Remember when I said I would set my author brand aside for practically everything else in life. Well, what can I expect? Not a million sales when my efforts are neither clear nor consistent. When you are not counting on the sales as part of your income, it is easy to be complacent. In the Marine Corps, as a military police officer, the mantra was "Complacency Kills". There it was meant to remind people if they tried to leave their bullet proof vest off because it was hot, or if they only put one set of handcuffs on their belt because it was heavy, it could result in serious damage if not loss of life if you needed those things among a dozen other warnings ranging from, "Don't turn your back, interview anyone in a kitchen (hello knives), or neglect to report your location before getting out of a car".

Complacency kills your author brand too. I am at this point, resurrecting a brand. Not just one book, but an entire brand with multiple series and so much that I could have been working these past 14 years. It is shameful really, but that is how this came about. It is time for you to learn from my shame because the whole time I have been neglecting my author brand, I have been supporting and encouraging and aiding others as they built theirs.

I'm not going to tell you what works in this section. I am going to tell you what I know for a fact is not the best way to do things because this is how I have been doing them.

1. Release a book with little to no warning.
2. Don't bother to understand that there are algorithms on social media
3. Don't worry about promoting it
4. Don't ask anyone to help you
5. Continue to promote people who are NOT helping you
6. Why bother tracking sales?
7. Who cares about other platforms?
8. Spend as little time in marketing hell as possible and wonder why nothing works
9. Avoid studying those actually selling to determine what they are doing right
10. Treat the author in you like a hobby rather than a part time job but expect it to perform like a full-on career when you need it to.
11. Why bother with a website? I mean social media rules all, right?

12. No one reads newsletters anymore, but everyone still uses e-mail, so…
13. Post random shit in no consistent fashion
14. Create random shit and post that in even less consistent fashion
15. Get lazy with covers (Hello, I love My Marine series)
16. Forget about some of your titles…I wrote that?
17. Avoid updating anything
18. Avoid changing with the times
19. Lie to yourself
20. Pretend it doesn't matter…when you know damn good and well it does.

In the words of the musical artist, Lizzo, "Truth Hurts." Which is why after coming to accept, admit, and embrace my truth I can move on to "Feelin' Good as Hell."

You will need to figure out your own strategy, but what I know for sure is that you must have one and you must actually execute that plan to completion if you have any chance of understanding if it will work.

The year of writing began for me out of need rather than want. I had big plans and major changes on the horizon and a whole year to figure it all out and get it all done. Part of that plan was already in progress. We purchased a home in the mountains. This did a couple of very personal things for us that I am making public in this book.

1. A major one for me is that I am within a 6-hour drive to my adoptive parents in Kentucky. I did not want to move back to Kentucky, but I did want to be closer. We now have the ability to use a large airport and take a 1 plane trip to Connecticut, Kentucky, Arizona, Nevada, Califor-

nia, Alabama, South Carolina, and Wyoming (maybe one stop on that route). Part of the retirement goal after twenty-plus years of military movement was to be able to get to family, friends, and the Raiders easier and with less expense. Note: Yes, I said Raiders, if that is a problem for you just stuff it deep down and don't let it impact the rest of this book for you. Unless you are also a Raider's fan, I don't like your team either and I am still trying to help you. If you by chance have no idea what I am talking about, it's NFL football.

2. Chris, my husband, has always wanted to live in the mountains and wanted all four seasons. I could personally do without winter, but it comes with the territory. After multiple deployments and the desire to be a little more "remote", this location worked for us.

The thing is, we thought we were going to have a full year to get this cabin in the woods settled while we also got the house along the coast ready for sale. We went back and forth on when exactly we would move or when I would move, but ultimately, the United States Coast Guard made the decision for us when they cut funding to the contract I was working. Now, I have no bad words for them. I loved my time there and the job. In fact, with that pretty high debt degree (PhD) in higher education administration, I sort of saw it coming. My PhD senses were tingling the same way they did when they combined the Writing and Reading program at a college I was working at several years before.

After that first government furlough in 2018, I knew budget issues were looming. Such is the life of a contractor. I told them when I took the job, if I could get at least two solid years of working full-time in one job it would be amazing. At the time, I was teaching for four, yes four, different higher education institutions. Two online and two in person. The downsizing came two months short of two years, but it was a very good two years of having only one "day" job to worry about.

A smart author would have taken advantage of that one job to worry about and maximized the time. I didn't. I was still not looking at my author brand as a source of any real income, but I did figure out if I put a little more into it I could offset the cost of an event I attend annually. My goal became earning enough money to cover the cost of that event. What is surprising is with some focus and drive; I was able to do that.

This is the moment when I realized that my author brand wasn't a poor performer because the books weren't popular enough. It was because I wasn't working any angle hard enough or consistently enough. I did this to my brand. I neglected it and it faded away. I started to pay attention and it began to show signs of life. Not many things in this world will do that for you. The entertainment industry is filled with that story line, but for every Robert Downy Junior there is a…I don't know because they aren't working anymore.

My recommendation for any writer reading this book is to consider some of these things because it is never too late in the entertainment industry. If you were unaware, that is exactly where we are, in the entertainment industry. Therefore, if you have faded away, it is time to resurrect yourself. If you market it right, like a true masochist, maybe you can get to orgasm or a million sales. I don't know which would feel better, but I know that the million sales will last longer, and you can publicly brag about it.

Here is the list of things to consider:

1. No matter what you write or what name you write under, if you publish it and any one person purchases it, that is a part of your legacy. Good, bad, or indifferent, you are leaving a piece of art out there for someone to discover long after you have left this plane of existence.

2. Have some sort of plan for that inevitable outcome. I have a will and there are specific directions for what is to happen to the work I have published by that point and what is and is not to happen to work I have written (typed or hand) that was not published by that point.

3. After you have considered the end of your life and what will happen to your writing you can start with the end in mind and think about what kind of writer, author, you really want to be known as.

4. With that honest lens you are looking through, figure out what kind of time and attention you can realistically give to your author brand.

My Brand Plan

Activity	Realistic Time I can Give	DIY or Outsource	3 Month Checkpoint
Writing Stories			
Editing			
Website			
Social Media Posts (general)			
Contest/Giveaways			
Uploading for Audio			
Listening to Auditions			
Listening to final productions			
Promoting Audio			
Book Cover Design			
Graphic Design			
Formatting Interior for e-book			
Formatting Interior for print			
Writing blurbs and hooks			
Writing promotion posts			
All other Copy			

This is just a list to get you started. You can add to the rows or scratch out the parts that don't apply to you. I put in the Do It Yourself (DIY) and Outsource column because there are times it may benefit you more to pay someone else to do some of these things.

Common misconceptions about having a virtual assistant (VA) is that they are full-time. While that is an option, there are plenty of VAs working part time or specializing in task based options, so as your writing business grows and you can begin to employ people, look at it as a good thing.

BDSM and the Writer: It's not what you think

BDSM stands for Bondage/Discipline, Dominance/Submission, and Sadism/Masochism. It became widely thrown around after an author wrote some adult fan fiction based on a teen book series and bam! Everyone and my mother suddenly know what BDSM is and not only are they talking about it, it's cool. I don't have any qualms with the BDSM community. I write several books that include the more common and less aggressive sexual elements of it. I do not, I repeat, I do NOT practice this lifestyle in my personal relationship. I do not have anything against it, but there is a lot more than you read in books that takes place in that lifestyle and quite frankly beyond fiction, I don't have an interest in it. Why am I telling you this? I don't want people to e-mail me and ask. Because out of everything in the book, this is the kind of stuff people get off track thinking about.

What I can say about BDSM is that the terms can be applied beyond the lifestyle of clubs and bedrooms across the globe. As a writer, especially one seeking publication, you enter into this contract with yourself and the world that is pretty much filled with these elements minus the sex.

Being a writer takes discipline, and you are bound to whatever story is coursing through you at that time. If you are not bound or disciplined, all of it will go away. That is the punishment. The loss of ideas and inspiration if you do not obey. Now, it may not be your fault. Your "Master" or in my case "Muse" may come calling when you are driving 80 miles per hour (MPH) down I-95 and you can't very well pull over and start writing without risking your life. Maybe it comes knocking right as you get the shampoo in your hair, or when you are waking up from sleep and trying your best to grasp the thoughts, or when you are falling asleep and can't believe you won't remember it in the morning (but you rarely do). It's a real pain in the ass and yet if you are a writer, you stay in this relationship with your Muse, you keep going back for more, promising to remember next time. Doing your best to do just that.

Next, is the Dominance and Submission element of being a writer. You are going to battle this at times. Everyone wants to be in control of the thoughts in your own head. As a writer, when you are in the dominant role it's all, "Characters will do what I tell them when I tell them!"

Then you will experience the reality of submission. Your characters say, "Okay, that sounds good, but this sounds better. Maybe this character needs a bit more, this one a little less..." This will go on and on for your entire writing life.

Sometimes you will be the one in charge and things will go as you planned without any additional sidetracks, new characters, ideas, plots, twists, turns, etc. Then, other times you will have planned out this beautiful story and then when you start to write, you won't be able to stay on plan and be satisfied with that content if someone gave you a million bucks for it.

You could probably write it, but it would sit there, looking at you from your bookshelf, calling you a sell-out, telling you it could have been better if only. Then you will have to remember you got paid a million dollars and say something snarky like, "That's right book, I did sell out, that's what paid for the shelf you're sitting on. Shut up!" Note: Yes, I do imagine you will be crazy in this scenario. I never imagined any author as a hundred percent sane, ever.

I mean, I'm not telling you to avoid a million-dollar book because your characters are fighting for the reins. Write that book! I'm just telling you this is what happens sometimes. You have control over the story one day, you don't the next. The Dom/Sub relationship between you and your Muse or you and your characters is one you will have to constantly negotiate. Through that negotiation you might find compromise between what you planned and what the story revealed itself to be. It's a strange process. You may not believe me.

You might not have come across this…yet. The writing process is an art and each artist will process their craft as they learn it and fine tune it. Unless I am working on a story that is part of a themed anthology, a guest spot, or an actual article for a non-fiction outlet, I let my characters run the show.

My books play out like movies in my head and I just do my best to keep up. I could create a writing practice of putting in time every day, but sometimes that is not enough. Sometimes if I don't stay longer the words, the scene, will escape me, change, shift the entire story on me. I try my best to start writing a story and go, go, go until it is done. I would love to be the person that can turn it on and off in a timed fashion. I am getting better at that, but it has taken me years of practice (over 14 and still counting) learning how to pause that movie reel and to be able to pick up where it left off. If you are the Dom, always, my suggestion would be to explore life as a Sub sometimes. If you are the Sub in your writing life, sign on to a project that makes you stick to the plan now and then just to show yourself you CAN. Again, this type of D/S situation applies only to your writing. I have no preference for knowing your situation anywhere else so please do not send me e-mails about it.

I've already touched on the Sadism and Masochism elements of being a writer in the previous essay Marketing is for Masochists. Writers are a bit sadistic. I mean really, we do take some pleasure from putting others through pain. What character is not better for the tortures we put upon them? The hero's journey is a journey through obstacles not a journey of smooth sailing. All our lives are filled with moments of challenge and we usually feel better on the other side of that challenge. We often sit around thinking about what would make this character's life really hell until we fix it for them to be better…or worse.

This doesn't mean you get to do that in real life, but there are a LOT of published authors out there that feel entitled to making other people feel as if their work is not as good, is not worthy, is not up to whatever standard those narcissists have set. DO NOT, I repeat, do not listen to them. Every book has an audience. You may be writing something new or on the fringe of a genre or on the fringe of a fringe genre. It is your story; you write it the way you want to. There are books out there, published, that are composed of text messages, books with pictures of animals with bubble captions that have misspelled words because…animals can't spell? I don't know.

I do know that some people were probably telling them that is not a thing, and now, those things are all over the place and those authors are making money off those books. You write your books! Don't let other authors be your critics unless they are people you trust. People you trust should say things like, "A five-hundred-page chapter is a little out of the norm, maybe break it into several." It will be actual advice to help you improve your writing. Don't be lured into the pit of despair by those authors who get off on making other authors feel small, and whatever you do, don't buy their books! If someone cannot support you, you have no reason to support them.

Also, do not become one of those people. I would hope the person reading THIS book is the kind of person who has empathy for others, values the diversity of our world, and appreciates that not all art is created and consumed by the same people. We all have target markets, and nothing is meant for everyone. It doesn't have to be. If you don't like my language, the sarcasm, the approach to writing, that is okay. This is not the book for you. If you are this far into it, I'm pretty sure you are with me, getting some value from it, and not likely to be a dick to other writers just because you can.

Now, on to the M. It is not just for marketing. You're entire writing career will likely be filled with ups and downs so the masochist in you will keep coming back because the pain is nothing compared to the pleasure. The aching wrists, the carpal tunnel syndrome, the dry eyes, new prescriptions every year, special screen prescriptions, the reminder that you MUST get up, stretch and move about because you are trapped in front of a computer for this job. It is not glamorous. It is not practical, and it is not free of its pains, so why do we do it?

Well, we are on our own hero's journey. As much as you love torturing your characters so they can feel elated at their victories, the universe enjoys torturing artists so we can appreciate and value every book sold with joy in our hearts. Unless it is like a ton of purchases that joy is not about all the compensation you are going to get. Just sayin'. I'm trying to keep it real with you. Some of you will make a lot of money, some of you will not. All of you will probably keep writing. That's the M.

Book Signings

You have your book in print and you are ready to go out in the world, sit at a table, and sell it. Celebration time all around!

Get past that. You have a lot of work to do. Book signings are a tradition for authors, and we love getting behind that table, meeting our readers, talking about our characters. That is also a bit of a delusion of grandeur. Until you have enough books out, you are a household name, or your readership is following you to every signing event you book, you are more likely to encounter this scenario instead.

You set up your table, people walk past you. Some of them will take any free promotional stuff you have, you know the Stuff We All Get (SWAG), and of those people a quarter of them will actually talk to you or ask for it. The other seventy-five percent will just smile, grab, and go, barely if even, making eye contact with you. They don't want to talk to you. They do not want to hear your pitch. They want your SWAG. As tempting as it may be to give these particular guests the stink eye, train your expression. You never know if they are going to turn into your readers. They are often referred to as "Treasure Hunters" and the term is not used kindly in most author circles. However, as a bit of a dragon myself, I don't have any problems with them. In fact, if you brought stuff to give away, to get your brand out there for any and all to see, you need these treasure hunters to pick it up, otherwise you become a hoarder of your own promotion materials and the only people who see it are your loyal reads and the cycle of your circle not growing continues because you don't want to give your ink pens to people who don't buy your book. See how that gets crazy really quick?

I have author friends on both sides of this debate. It is way more interesting than most political debates so if you ever get to see one, tune in. I will discuss a little more about promotional materials in another chapter, so you can tune in there if you prefer, research, and come to your own conclusions for your own brand, but for now, we are just talking about your book signing.

Once the hunters have passed, you will get the "Inquiring Potentials". These are readers actually there to pick up new books from new authors, but they likely have a budget and you have to convince them your book is worth parting with those limited funds. This is the reason you absolutely MUST have a pitch for your book or series. You have less than a minute to say hello, ask what they read, and then tell them what you have to offer. Before you get to a book signing, you need to become a pitcher.

Just like the Major League Baseball (MLB) player pitching for a professional team, you will need to practice and practice, and pitch to everyone, and anyone that falls within your target market. There is a section on pitches. Read that before you go to a signing.

I know you are thinking, are you serious? When does the sales come in?

Right now, impatient.

Once you have either converted that Inquiring Potential, or you have been approached by an Auto Buyer (you love this reader), you get to make the sale. Purchasing customers get more than just your book. You should always have an extra for those people, and only those people. It might be a sticker, a handmade bookmark, the ink-pen if you have paper products for the hunters to pick up. The more they buy, the more they get.

Now, you are thinking, what the actual fuck? I have to give them more than just my book? No, you do not have to do this. I am suggesting that you do this. Why? Because it gives a little more of a personal touch, it gives them one more thing to take with them to talk about or take a picture of when they share their purchase information later with friends or (please, please) on social media. If you are good to paying readers, especially at events, they are often good to you by sharing your brand through their channels when they post about it. That is advertising, people and they do not have to do that since it is the best and most valuable kind of advertising: consumers selling product through endorsement or review. You spend less on that item than you would for that kind of promotion, so think about it.

This is all budget based. You must plan for that and there is a section in this book for those plans, too. None of these other sections make sense without this part coming first. Otherwise it's all, blah, blah, track this, get that. Now, because you read this you realize that sitting at a table alone or with another author on the other half of said table, you must be ready to face your audience, your readers, and everyone else walking by or up to you. Seems super easy, but only if you plan for it. Otherwise, you sit there and look at everyone else and think, I should have…, I wish I…, Why didn't I think of…?

Part of the purchase of this book is the fact that you don't have to think of everything, I have had plenty of embarrassing moments at book signing to prevent you from having as many. You may still have your share of them, but hopefully, less.

The upcoming pages are filled with information about signings and a small section about expos. Several events have the term expo in the name but are not, in fact, an expo. This does not mean you should avoid them; it just means you need to know what you are getting into. Is it a signing with expo in the name because it is larger than usual, but not filled with booths, or it is an expo which means you need to be prepared to dress an entire space and bring a staff of people with you to represent your brand.

Questions to Ask About a Book Signing

Here are things you want to know about a book event and things they should be able to provide to you:

1. Date and time of event
2. Time authors can get in and set up
3. Place of event
4. Date of event (I know that is obvious, but you would be surprised at "upcoming" advertisements with no set date)
5. How long has the event been going on?
6. What is the amount of foot traffic?
7. What genres are accepted?
8. What is the breakdown of genres at the event? (If it is 90% Sci-Fi and you have an Amish romance, you can scale back your expectations very easily)
9. What is the average amount of books sold? (This will vary by author, but if they are doing an exit survey, they should have some idea of the authors that did well and those who did not and the middle number.)
10. What was the age range of attendees? (Again, if a lot of families come in you may not sell more explicit, violent, horror type titles, at least not that day.)
11. If it is outdoor, what is provided and what is the inclement weather plan? (if you need shade you need to know if tents are provided) Everyone needs to know if tables and chairs are provided or if you need to bring your own.
12. What is the space allotted?
13. What is the cleanup like? Now if this is a bookstore, you won't have any, but if it is an outdoor event hosted by the library, you need to know if they will provide trash receptacles and if security will be there to ensure no one tries to "help you" breakdown your tables. Sometimes people won't leave and there has been a weird trend in people offering to "help" for a

fee and being aggressive about it. You need to be sure your space is secure.

14. What is the bathroom situation (again, more important if the event is outside)?
15. Will food or snacks be provided or available nearby for purchase? (I've attended events with both situations).
16. Do you have to pay for an additional person to be at the table with you?

If there is food provided, ask if they have an assistant rate (usually less because that person is just getting access and eating) because you will need to pay for that person. There is no "share" when it comes to food at these events. If two people are eating, then you need to pay for two meals.

Note: If you are at an outdoor event, even if it is for 3 hours, I suggest taking a person able to sit at the table and tell people you will be right back should you need to go to the bathroom. You cannot rely on the other vendors to take care of your stuff if you suddenly have a situation. They have their own business to run and won't miss a sale to guard your stuff, nor should they, nor should you for anyone else. Most places do not charge for you to have an assistant as long as that assistant is there to help you set up and take down, or just there at your table, not consuming anything meant for paying vendors.

Packing Checklist for Book Signing

- ☐ Signing Box*
- ☐ Banner(s)
- ☐ Signing Pen
- ☐ SWAG and containers for SWAG to remain neat
- ☐ Special SWAG (for those who purchase)
- ☐ Book Stand
- ☐ Price Board
- ☐ Books (seriously, don't forget the books!)
- ☐ Credit card reader
- ☐ Cash for change
- ☐ Snack
- ☐ Water
- ☐ Mints
- ☐ Clipboard with attached pen
- ☐ Sign-up sheet
- ☐ A mat to stand on (especially if outside on concrete)
- ☐ Identify a runner
  - notify that person
- ☐ _____
- ☐ _____
- ☐ _____
- ☐ _____
- ☐ _____
- ☐ _____
- ☐ _____
- ☐ _____
- ☐ _____
- ☐ _____
- ☐ _____
- ☐ _____

*Signing Box is the box you put most, if not all, of this stuff in. Think of a sturdy footlocker with a handle and on wheels. A lot of people use luggage.

Be sure to attach the pen to the clipboard or you will continually replace it. Might seem like a good idea until you must stop talking to a paying reader to give a pen to a treasure hunter.

A Bit About Expos

According to the dictionary it is a "large exposition". No shit, right? Well, you may be surprised at how many book signings use the term expo for events with less than 100 authors. Additionally, the term expo suggests more pomp and circumstance than the average book signing. Expos are typically selling products and experiences, think of a bridal expo when you walk under an arch at every booth, get cake samples, and hear music as you get closer to the table. These are product-based events where there is a lot of interaction with the things and environment that display has established. Book expos are often larger than life with characters, dramatic displays, etc. Think *Book Expo America.*

Wondering if it is a signing or an expo? For an event to be an expo it typically has these common features:

1. There are hundreds (at least 100) booths set up for vendors. Yes, you do sign books there, but the massive amount of people, vendors, and time constraint for them to see the 100 plus other vendors means limited time and connection. It does mean maximum exposure, if you can get someone to at least take some promo.

2. You are going to pay a chunk of money, not including registration, because you will need to have enough promotion material to go around (think thousands).

3. You will also need to save up for the hotel and such because Expos typically happen in large cities. I say this because your local chamber of commerce may run a small business expo and it can vary in size and it will be similar to the larger expos, but it is NOT the kind of expo that will lure new people in from other states and areas. Similar theme, but different scale.

If you look at major expos you will see that the photos advertising them are of vast rooms (usually major conference centers) filled with booths and passageways filled with people.

I attended Book Expo America in New York a long time ago on behalf of a publisher. While it was okay, and we gave out a lot of promotion material (there was a team of us) the majority of the crowd back then was not interested in small press. We were on the second floor along a hallway which meant a lot of people passed the section, but it was not comfortable for them to stop for long as it was essentially a hallway. Even the "vendors" in the larger spaces were missing people because the sheer volume does not lend for a lot of docking time. The people attending need to get to as many places as they can to see as much as possible in that limited time. I don't regret doing it, but I would not do it on my own.

Please beware of events that have the name EXPO in them but are not actually an expo. It sounds good to say this is an expo, but look carefully and determine if it is in fact an expo or just a signing, or is it a convention, or is it just an event? It is your responsibility to figure that out. The event planners may be marketing their event wrong, but you are ultimately the one deciding to pay for it so make sure you talk to people who have been there and determine if it is worth it.

The booths at an expo are almost an experience themselves. Most signing and conventions DO NOT have the space or resources for you to set up your fictional world for guests to step into. If you're at a hotel, you are probably just going to have a table and maybe only half of one. That part of it is just a signing. Could be a nice one, but it is still a signing. If you are at a convention center for an expo, you need a small staff with you to manage that booth.

Additionally, timing is everything. If you contact a hotel or convention center and the event staff don't know what you are talking about, don't give anyone money until a manager there does (every clerk may not be aware of an event 6 months out, but a manager or the event staff should). If an event of any type is advertising a location for rooms, the staff there should know an event is coming. Unfortunately, as an indie author you are vulnerable to people who think it is okay to tell you they are hosting a book signing or expo or convention and then they take your money and cancel the event leaving you to find out there never was an event, a hotel agreement, or an actual person with that name. I saw it happen twice in 2018 and once in 2019 and that is all one time too many. I'm sure it happened more, but those incidents impacted people I knew.

Protect yourself.

Notes

Questions to Ask Before Expo Registration

Ask all the same questions that apply to the setting for a book signing and add these:

1. What is included in the cost of registration? (How many people to run the booth?)
2. Do you have a room block at a hotel with a discount? What is the contact info and rates?
3. Will you provide recommendations for hotels and airports if you do not have a contract with a hotel already in place?
4. What is the refund policy?
5. Who are the points of contact and what are their roles? (An expo is rarely run with one single POC).

Book Conventions

Conventions are not for people interested in selling books because a lot of readers will be there. Those convention readers are not the same as book signing readers. Sure, they also go to signings, but when they are at a convention, paying to be there, paying for your time, they expect to get it. If you do not spend time with them before that book signing event, they will not spend money on you.

Literary Love Savannah is the event I invest in as an author. I do that because I have been a part of the event in some capacity since it began as Authors After Dark over 12 years ago. The event has evolved with the industry and the readers are more invested than ever in the authors investing in them. There are multiple reader and author gatherings that have been taking place annual or semi-annually for well over a decade. This committed readership attending the event(s) of choice is not unique to Literary Love Savannah. Several events have popped up across the nation and it is important for you to research, talk to authors, look at reviews, talk to your readers, and see what will work for you.

Most of the ones, including LLS that I recommend or support have been running for well over ten years, have volunteer staffs, contribute to some local non-profit organization, and keep cost low by not turning a profit off of registrations.

There is nothing wrong with event planners earning money from planning events. Please do not read that wrong. I believe event planners should get paid. I don't think authors planning events so they can make money off their fellow authors and attending readers through registration and signing table sales should get significantly paid for it unless they are truly event planners. If they plan weddings, birthdays, and book signings, cool. That is a job. They probably have a card and website for event planning services. If they are planning an event because they want to make a quick, significant profit on indie authors seeking a space to sign, that's not cool. Those people are exploiting them/us. It may not be a popular opinion, but if you are reading this book, you are likely going to look for places to sign your books. Chose wisely. Ask questions. Again, someone (even an author hosting an event) earning a reasonable profit for the work, okay. Earning little or no profit and raising money for a charitable cause, even better.

Someone earning lots of profit, and you get little benefit for what you pay them, not okay. Just my view.

That is why I made this list of questions for you to ask.

Convention Questions

In addition to the information you asked about a signing and/or expo, add these to any event labeled as a convention.

1. What sponsorship opportunities will there be?

    Sponsoring everything from SWAG at a meal table to providing snacks before the book signing is important for the event and for you. Your name goes on that sponsorship. Readers know you did more. They tend to give more sales to those who provide more experiences to them.

2. Is there a Social Media marketing plan and or a traditional marketing plan in place?

    Some events have a plan in place already and some let you free style. Either way, you need to promote that event like it is yours because you want readers you KNOW are coming to see you. You need readers to be at these events for you. They are your brand ambassadors. The ones who spread the good word to other readers in a non-sales way because they are not making a hard sale for you. They are simply saying, I paid to be here to see (insert your name here). The conversation flows naturally from there. If the event does not have a marketing plan in place, maybe that can be your contribution. Review the event to see if it is one ran by volunteers (like LLS) or if it is one charging you for staff and other labor in the cost of your admission. Every event should be able to disclose what your admission is paying for. If the staff is turning a profit, they should also be coming up with the advertising dollars to promote their own event.

3. Is there a mentor program?

   If there is, get in it and ask all the questions you want to someone that attends the event rather than winging it. They have been there, done this, knew if it was successful for them. Listening to those techniques should also work for you.

4. Is this a for-profit or non-profit event?

   The only reason you need to know this is so you can measure your own expectations of what you are paying for. If they are making money off your registration, they need to be doing a lot more work **for** you than just providing a seat at a table. If they are not making a dime and providing a space for you to be an artist, **you** need to be doing a lot more work for you to be successful at the event.

What works for you?

There are several factors to determine if an event was a success. Keep in mind that just because it was a successful event, doesn't mean it was the event for you. If you were miserable more than not but sold out, you may have to decide if the sales were worth whatever else you had to endure.

My example of an event of such nature is simple. I used to attend a local (to where I lived at the time) book signing and it was held in a building, but there was no heat. It was freezing two years in a row and when it came to the third year, I said no because I also didn't have access to an outlet where I could hook up a space heater. Most of the authors dressed in winter clothes and were fine, but I get cold very quickly and it makes me miserable.

I sold books, recouped the cost and then some, but the physical discomfort for the 1 ½ hour we had to be there before the event opened plus the 4 hours of the event was just 5 ½ hours of cold. It was not worth it for me to be miserable for that amount of time.

In this case, I had to figure out what that event did right, but also find one with those elements that makes me less miserable. I primarily look for events locally in Spring and Summer, or if it is in Fall and Winter I ask if the space has central air and heat.

Most authors will have one main factor, money. How much do you have to spend on an event? What is your annual or quarterly budget?

I spent several years of my undergraduate program as a sales manager and what I learned during that time is that those numbers matter. My budget in that role was for employee hours and the only way to increase hours during a season that was budgeted for less was if they were increasing sales. No way to justify it otherwise.

Something similar may happen to you on the event circuit. You may look at your annual budget, look at the events offered, and then look at the amount you would have to sell in order to recoup the cost of the event and then think you can't afford to attend anything!

Here is the truth about events, you may not earn back what you put out at the event. Look at the cost of your books, the registration, the hotel, extras, promo, etc. and then decide how you want to approach and track sales, but more importantly how you want to measure success.

Is success selling out of books even if it doesn't cover the entire cost of the event? Is success reaching more people even if you don't sell out of books? Is success getting through the event in one piece? It all depends on you, your goals, and how you plan to measure success. It is easier to recoup the cost of a book signing because you are paying for the space at the table and what you put on it (books and merchandise for sale).

Another aspect of these events are the sales you make leading up to the event if you are active on social media (SM) and in SM groups and talking to those readers. There are the sales you make at the event. Then there are the residual sales you make in the month or two after the event (remember all those treasure hunters we talked about, they just looked at your SWAG). You will not know, other than the ones you sell live at the event, if all those other sales are a result of the event, but you should be able to notice a trend in sales before and after every event.

Marketing is not always a clear "pay for this" and see immediate results. Readers that don't buy from you year one at an event might buy every title you have year two. Unless the event was a complete disaster, you may need to make the investment a couple years to see the returns. Convention going readers are already committed to being there, interacting, and if they have taken the time to do all of that, you have to show up, participate, and invest your time so they feel comfortable handing over their money.

Money is a huge part of your platform as an author. I'm not going to get into legal and tax stuff here, but it is important that you at least start to learn what you are responsible for as a business. If you are selling books, even if you think it is a hobby, the authorities may think otherwise. Especially, if your hobby takes off faster than you thought it would and you start earning a steady income from it. That is not a hobby. That is a business, so know your basics.

Aside from the financial and business aspects of an event, you should feel comfortable there, welcomed. If the people hosting it and the other authors attending it are putting on a convention version of the movie *Mean Girls*, chances are that is not an event you want to be a part of. You do NOT have to attend anything. You do NOT have to give anyone your money. If you chose to sign up, the least they can do is provide a welcome environment.

Now that I have told you the event needs to be welcoming, let me remind you that you are not the only author there, not the only new author there, and not the only one with questions and needs. Most of those you should ask before you give them your money to ensure it is right for you. There is nothing worse than a new author high on AUTHOR STATUS. Even if you are a lister, as in you hit the best-selling list somewhere, you are not special at a book signing. This means they aren't either. Unless they paid more. If you pay more, then yes, you get the best table, you get to sit near the outlet so you can charge your phone, and yes, you probably have top billing on the event attendee list. They PAID for that. It wasn't given to them because they are special. It was an investment that author made in the event in order to showcase their brand.

I remember as a young, new, naïve author congratulating someone on making the cover of the then popular romance reader magazine. She smiled and said, "Well, I paid enough for it. I hope it makes a difference in my sales for this new release or I just wasted a bunch of money." It was then I realized that this New York Times and USA Today Bestselling author of multiple books that hit those charts was having the same author concerns that I was, but on a different financial scale. If you need press there are two ways to get it, but in the end, none of it will set you apart in the eyes of an event planner unless you are paying for big ticket items to happen at that event. You want to drop ten thousand dollars on snacks for the attending readers, yeah, someone is going to make sure you get a good table, and everyone knows you sponsored the snacks. If you want to pay one hundred and fifty dollars for your seat at a book signing, you are just going to get your space wherever they seat you.

Events don't fail authors as often as authors fail events. If you have left your career and sales in the hands of a stranger and then realize no one is attending this event, that is on you my author friend, not the event coordinator. Sure, they should be out selling that event everywhere, but so should you. If they have done their best to get the word out to the community and no one attends it means no one was interested in seeing any of you signed up to be there, or that none or not enough of you let people know you would be there. If you invested the money, why wouldn't you invest the time to let people know?

Final thoughts on is this for me include:
1. Financially viable (if it is a loss, can you take the loss?)
2. Emotionally fulfilling (enjoyable, welcoming, worth it)
3. Physically accessible (no freezing rooms for me)
4. Ethical (am I okay with how it is running, who can attend, etc.)

You have a lot of ways to measure if an event is successful and I can only offer you points to consider and think about before you hand your hard-earned money over to someone.

What else do I need for events?

My suggestion is to get a table banner that isn't much bigger than the width of a pillowcase. Why? Because you can always put that in the center of a 4-7 foot table if you have the table to yourself, but it will still work as a center banner if you have to or chose to share a table.

I have not known of any convention that asked you to bring your own table. Conventions are usually at a hotel and if they have exhibit space in an adjoining location, they still have tables they charge for. I have attended many outdoor book signings that required the author to bring their entire setup, table, chair(s), tent for shade, etc. Expos may be somewhere in between, meaning the convention centers may have regular tables, but real expos have vendors bringing in props and custom designed spaces and such, so they may not want or need those. Always be sure to ask.

Aside from your table banner, in addition to, or instead of, you can always choose to have a standing banner. There are a lot of different versions of these. From the horizontal ones that provide a backdrop, to the traditional ones you see just about everywhere. I'll share my point of view, but remember, it is about what works for you and if you only have the money for one set-up you want to make sure you get the most versatile options.

Banners come in a variety of styles at these events. My suggestion if you are operating on a budget is to do an author banner rather than a book banner. I say this because you should have more than one book at some point, but if you can only buy one banner it can only advertise what you put on it at the time. Think long term use and your choices may seem less flashy than everyone else, but you won't have to buy a new banner every time you release a new book. Another reason to avoid putting book covers on banners is that your cover may change at some point which would then render it useless. Get creative. An author recently mentioned that she got a banner with her logo at the top and then attached her covers to the rest of it with Velcro so she could interchange them based on where she was and what she was selling. Others I know will do a banner for a series or genre of titles they write. It is still general enough to work for whatever book in that series or whatever book in that genre is their newest release. Take some time to plan and try to get to some events so you can see what you like as a reader. That will help you decide what you want to present as an author.

If you are going to a signing, expo, or convention that has been around a year or more, the best way to plan for it is to take an hour and scour the web for images related to the event. You will likely see a lot of group photos, but you, as the author, are looking for banners, table set-ups, costumes, general attire, those things. Depending on your personality and what you are comfortable with you can blend in or stand out on purpose.

You're going to the event! Hooray. Now what?

Ask if they will have Welcome Bags. Every convention and some signings I have attended offer welcome bags. Signing are usually limited to the first (insert amount) of people to enter, but conventions have a welcome bag for every attendee and that is given at the welcome event. Conventions know that it is a huge part of the marketing strategy and attendees expect a fabulous welcome bag.

Things to ask of the event:
1. How many items should I bring?
2. Are there restrictions?

Things to think about in general:

1. What do you have on hand left over from other events? Unless someone at the event says it must be the same item, you can put together what you have. If it requires 300 pieces of promotion material and you have 50 pens from one event, 25 from another, 70 stickers, and 200 stress balls, well you are already over 300 items.

2. Can you make something? If you have 500 bookmarks, go to the store and get those big bags of mixed candy, put them in another little bag with the bookmark or attached to it somehow.

3. If it is an adult crowd think of putting your logo on: snacks, water, tissue, hand sanitizer, pens, pins, earplugs, lipbalm, sunscreen, nail files, mini sewing kits, and any other thing you always forget when packing for a trip.

4. If you would be exited to get it, so would someone else.

Table SWAG:
1. Table SWAG comes in 2 forms. The stuff you put out that anyone can pick up and walk away with even if they don't look at you when they take it, or talk to you at all, and the other stuff you give to people purchasing your book.

2. If you have paper bookmarks, put those on the table for everyone to get. If you got a steal on some ink-pens or something, yes, put those out. However, if you have paper bookmarks and ink pens and those are all you could afford. Paper is for everyone; pens are for payers. Level all your SWAG like that. If you have paper and ink pens for everyone, then the t-shirt, or jar opener is for those who purchase.

3. Never charge for SWAG. Bookmarks, unless custom or handmade, are considered SWAG. Lip-balm, nail files, pretty much anything you purchased in bulk is considered SWAG. You want as many people to take this home as possible because:

   a. You don't want to carry it back with you (unless you are saving it for next year's welcome bags) and
   b. Even if they don't buy from you then, they may look you up later. I had an ink-pen for almost a year before I picked it up, looked at the author, looked her up and yes, I bought a book. If I didn't have that pen a year later, she wouldn't have that sale or any of the others I made after it.

Merchandise is not SWAG. Merchandise, commonly referred to as merch, is the stuff people need to pay for.

Common author merchandise includes:

- Books: Your number one item.
- Items you have made: Custom bookmarks like the leather ones or metal ones. Think the stuff you would buy in a store, but you made it and it probably has a design or something related to your brand.

Note: Put something related to your band on your merch but be careful with putting your brand as the main thing on it. I mean, do you want a leather bookmark with someone else's brand on it? Probably not, but if you write about dragons and it has a hand drawn dragon or dragon and book title, yeah you might like that. Put your ego aside and let people represent your words and the places in them. I often wear a shirt with a club logo on it and when people ask where that is, I tell them in a book by Stella Price. Often, the reaction is, that's cool. Yes, it is! Anyone can get into that club when they buy the book and read the story.

- Small batch items you have ordered: Again, customized and limited editions. If you want them to pay it must be special.

- Also, if you are a crafter and make pottery, jewelry, candles, etc. related to your books or not, you might put a few of those out for sale. Just be sure to list them on a price board so people don't think they are free.

Create Deal Bundles where you can. If you have a series, offer a deal for buying the whole series. If not a price deal, then a bonus deal. A bonus would be one of the items above added to the series for free.

Example would be if you had a series where the main character is a chef, maybe you have a cute spatula or something that give away with the purchase of the whole series.

If you are at an event where you could allow people to pre-order, then you have to make sure you have a special something for them. This could be a handwritten thank you note, a coupon for them or a friend to use, a bag of chips and bottle water...tailor your bonus items to your event, but make sure if they pe-ordered, you have a special thank you for them.

Essentially, what I am trying to say here is that you need a lot of prep for a signing, but if you plan to be at a convention realize it is more than a signing and requires a time investment throughout the year. You should be planning and buying for it all year long.

Example: If you write holiday stories? The 75% off sale after the season is where you need to be buying anything blank you can sticker or logo for next year. Remember, you don't need 100 of them. Just enough to make the holiday bundle special.

Now that the SWAG and Merch is out of the way and you have a plan for that you must also include a few more things to prepare for your table.

You MUST:

1. Have a price board! At the very least some way for them to see what it costs so you don't repeat it over and over again.

2. Have a Square, PayPal, whatever card reader and test it before you get there to be sure it is working. If possible, preload your price points so you don't have to type it in or do the math when you have 3-4 people waiting, asking, and looking at your table. They have no idea you are trying to add something up in your head.

3. Have change. Most people try to sell things in bill format $5, $10, $15, $20, etc. because you don't have to make change. If you have a $6 book. You better be ready to give change if all they want is that book and all they have is a $20.

4. Have a runner. This is someone that can stand at your table in front or behind if you need to go to the bathroom mid signing. This is an assistant, a friend, a family member, or a trusted reader, who will grab you a drink because you already went through your two bottles of water. Identify this person early and have a plan. Otherwise, you rely on the author you share the table with or at the table next to you and they are probably going to say yes, but if a reader comes up to their table, their focus is naturally and rightfully going to shift to that reader.

Notes

Convention Q's to Ask Prior to Registration

Questions you need to ask before signing up for a convention in addition to knowing the book signing and expo info:

1. What sponsorship opportunities are there and what is the cost?
   - ☐ _____
   - ☐ _____
   - ☐ _____

2. Is there a Social Media marketing plan?
   - ☐ Yes (What are you required to do?)
     - • _____
     - • _____
     - • _____
     - • _____
   - ☐ No (your plan to overcome that if you still want to go)
     - • _____
     - • _____
     - • _____
     - • _____

3. Is there a mentor program?
   - ☐ Yes
     - • Mentor information
       _____
   - ☐ No (your plan to overcome that if you still want to go)
     - • _____
     - • _____

4. Is there a Welcome Bag? (If Yes):
   1. How many items should I bring? _____
   2. Are there restrictions? _____

Pitch Like You're Trying Out For MLB

There are all types of pitches you will need to master as an author. The most important pitch is the sales pitch at a book event. This is a short and simple summary of your work. It is your blurb in the verbal sense.

Reader: What are your books about?
Author:

This response will vary based on what you write. If you write multiple genres, you have about a minute or less to convey that so you can see what this reader is interested int. Don't ask a question as an answer, they don't like that. Would you like that?

Here are some sample responses:

Author 1: I write sci-fi, paranormal, and contemporary. Do you like any of those?

Author 2: I write historical romance based on real locations I've researched. Do you like historical?

Author 3: I write kick-ass heroines with paranormal heroes. What do you like to read?

Author 4: This is a non-fiction book based on my life as a nurse. Do you read memoirs?

Author 5: I write horror. Do you like horror?

Author 6: I write children's book with an emphasis on life lessons. Are you looking for a gift for someone special?

Answer with a general and true to your personality and brand and then ask a question. If you just answer and don't ask, they may walk away from you even if they do read your genre or content.

Reader: What is this book about?
Author:

This is a more specific question and it needs a specific response. They are not asking about all of your titles, they are not asking about you, they are asking what THIS book is about.

Here are some sample responses:

Author 1: Paranormal title is about main character's quest to find her brother who she suspects was stolen by another pack. It's the third book in series name. Do you like stories with werewolves?

Author 2: Historical title is about the Duchess of Location and Duke of Location which are both fictional characters I've placed in Castle Name which is a real place you can still visit if you are ever in England. Of course, you can travel back in time and see it through their eyes if you want to try out this book. Would you like to?

Author 3: Paranormal title is about kick ass heroine name and shifter hero as they battle enemy to save friend. Are you ready for the adventure?

Author 4: Nonfiction title is based on my years of experience as a specialty. If you would like to learn more about this field or you know a nurse, this is both a great read and an excellent gift idea. Would you like one?

Author 5: Horror title is about hero/monster/location and events that scare the shit out of you. Would you like a copy?

Author 6: Children's title is about characters and lesson appropriate for ages (start) and (finish). How many do you need?

Your closing must be sincere and authentic, and you will need to figure that out with practice. Don't judge a reader by the stack of books in hand. A reader may be buying all sorts of titles around that room, but they may not be for them. Some are gifts for others, so if you write horror and you see someone with a stack of historical romance in their hand it doesn't mean they won't buy your book. That stack may be for someone else, or your book may be for someone else, or ideally this is a diverse reader and one ready to buy books.

The biggest mistake authors make is forgetting that you are selling and not closing. If you speak to this person, they like your genre, they pick up the book, they ask what it is about, you answer some questions, they appear interested, they put the book back down and walk away, sometimes with a thank you, sometimes with an awkward acknowledgement. Just like you, they are not all extroverts who will close the sale for you with a "do you take credit cards?" They are not there to close your sales. They are there to find books. You are there to sell them.

Some lines to memorize and practice:

- Would you like for me to sign that copy to you or someone else?
- Is this for you or a friend?
- How many would you like?
- Would you like me to sign on the inside cover or on this page?

Now what if you have added on sales? If it is part of a series or you have this lovely merchandise you created for it, you don't want to let them get away without telling them about it. When do you bring this up? Not as an afterthought because then it may be too late.

Reader: I want this book.
Author:

Excellent, I want you to know that it is part of a series that I have a special price for in case you want to pick up the rest of them today.

Awesome, thank you. I also created these to go with it if you would be interested in one for (dollar amount). They are exclusive to (this event or book signings) so it is the only chance to grab one.

Thank you, I have the next book coming out in two months, would you like to sign up for my newsletter, so you don't miss the release date?

You don't have to ask for more sales. You just have to ask for whatever it is you are trying to get from that event. Are you building your newsletter? Do you send out cards for holidays and need mailing addresses? Do you want to increase your membership in your online group? All of those are added on features you need to include before you take the money or the credit card so you can have the correct total when you start, and if it is a sign-up they can do something while you process the sale.

I can't tell you how many times when I started out that I was so excited just to sell one book that I would not give them a chance to look at the others before I was already handling that sale. Sometimes they would buy the next one right then, but sometimes, they would have if I rang it all up at once, but since I didn't, they were off to the next thing with an, "I'll be back at the end if I still have money." Sometimes you see them, most of the time you don't.

It is a delicate balance between ensuring you gave your reader enough time to buy all they wanted from you in one stop and losing one sale because you are pushing them to add on to it. Again, this is about practice. If you have friends and family willing to role play with you, do that.

If not, then go to a store and observe the cosmetics counter carefully. They need two to three items per sale in order to stay on track for their performance review. When someone comes in to re-place a favorite lipstick it is a challenge to get them to buy one or two more things, but that is the goal. If you have more than one title or you have a book and merchandise, your goal is to sell more than one item at each sale. Will you? No, but you should try because each time you do you close the gap between how long it will take for you to re-coup what you put into this event financially. Additionally, the more accustomed you get to navigating the rejection of an added item, and ideally, the addition of added items, the easier and more natural it will be to handle both situations.

Practice your lines:

Interest:_____

_____

Closing:_____

_____

Add On:_____

_____

Networking Never Ends

Networking is not just what you do on your social media accounts. In fact, that is just one layer and possibly not even the most valuable one even if that is where people spend so much time trying to convince you to spend your marketing dollars. The truth is networks have layers. I'm sure you, like me, probably hear Mike Myers as Shrek talking about onions and ogres right now but stay with me! Marketing layers look a little something like this:

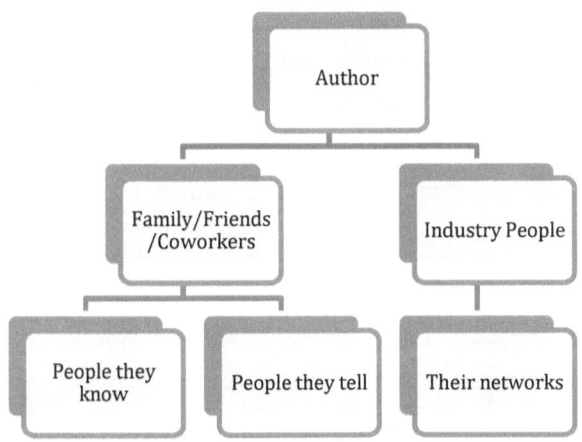

I know this is not what you expected to see. Where is all the social media and online content I should be talking about, right? Well, stick with me here. Online content is not separate from your network, it is simply a medium you and the people in your network use to connect to and with one another. It makes some things easier and some more challenging.

Who is in your network and what roles do they play in your craft?

Family: List all the family members who know you are an author. Highlight the ones who support you by buying your books and telling other people about them.

Friends: List all the friends (not other authors) who know you are an author. Highlight the ones who support you by buying your books and telling other people about them.

Co-workers: List all the co-workers who know you are an author. Highlight the ones who support you by buying your books and telling other people about them.

Industry People: Authors. Use different colors or create symbols to identify authors as friends, people who cross promote with you, people who you only work with on certain projects, and those who support you by purchasing your books or promoting your work.

Industry People: Everyone else. Use different colors or create symbols to identify people you pay and whether they purchase or promote your work after it is published.

Why does all of this matter? Because the people in your personal and professional life that purchase your books and promote them to others are people you need to be grateful for and people you need to make sure you are keeping in contact with. Do not take them for granted!

Also, if you are paying for editing services, cover art, graphics, etc. and that artist is not using it in their portfolio or promoting it, that may be an indicator that they are in it for the money and not supporting you. It may be worth it for some things, but you don't want to give any extra back to them. Why promote or refer a cover artist that doesn't post that they created a cover for you on their social media? If they don't do it for anyone, okay, but since covers are likely a part of their income it says something if they are not proud enough to share the work with their audience. I've edited a few things and I promote those books because I want that author to do well and send me new work to edit! Think about it that way. It is an income funnel here, you do well, you have money to buy more from them.

This is especially true of narrators. If a narrator read your book but doesn't have a plan to market the book that is an artistic expression of your work likely making them money with every sale, you may want to reconsider using that narrator in the future.

Good Review, Bad Review, and You

Reviews can make you feel like you are on the right path and your work is serving its purpose. They can also feel like a personal attack. They are neither of these things.

Reviews are other people's opinions of your work. You can find insight in well written reviews, but never stop writing just because someone doesn't like what you write.

Here is an excerpt from one of my favorite scathing reviews about Tequila Makes Her Clothes Fall Off: "My god was this book ever dumb :-/" It goes on like that for three and a half more paragraphs.

This next review was a 5-Star review of the same book: "I thoroughly enjoyed this sweet and erotic romance by Cara North. The hero and heroine were both genuinely nice people, and I enjoyed watching the relationship develop between them." It goes on like that for another three paragraphs, too.

It doesn't matter how many 5-Star reviews I have on this title, the "was this book ever dumb" comment made me wonder: Exactly what is a romance supposed to be? It took me a little bit to get past that reviewer's opinion of the book. It was the first book of mine to get published by a publisher. The joy of having a book published was quickly diminished by that review and became one reason I do NOT read reviews before I have completed and published all the books in a series. It can be paralyzing.

It's not just bad reviews you have to watch out for. If the reviews are too good, you might get what I call Harper Lee syndrome and worry the next book won't meet expectations. If the reviews are really bad, you might get worried that you should stop now while you are only getting beat up about one title.

It took me a few years to get to the point where I finally just decided that I didn't need to read the reviews until I was done with a series, because I didn't need to put myself through that roller-coaster for a bunch of other people I can't control. Did the reviewer that called my book dumb even consider me when she wrote it?

No, not likely. She didn't care what I thought, so why should I care what she thinks? If I let her negative comments overshadow everything I am working on in that series, I am disappointing myself, and the people who DID like the book.

The hardest thing for us to do is separate ourselves from the work. The review is happening to the book, the book is what she thinks is dumb. She didn't say Cara North is dumb, she essentially said, Cara North wrote something dumb. Plenty of really smart people write dumb pieces! I teach and preach to my writing students to not take a grade personally. It is the evaluation of the work not the person submitting it.

Once I was able to put a review in the perspective of a grade, it was easy to realize I can't write for every teacher (reader) out there because I don't have their rubric to make sure I hit all of the details they find important. If you write in academics, you need to see the grading rubric so you can be sure to hit all the parts of the assignment. As an author, you don't get these because they do not exist. No way can you predict what every person who picks up your book is going to think about it or what they expected to get from it. Once I had that settled in a way I could process it, then I was able to let go of it and now reviews don't bother me nearly as much as they used to if they are negative.

Additionally, using that academic lens to view my work through I could re-read these reviews and see what was valuable to me and my work. The reviewer hating the book gave examples for me to think about. While some of them were difficult for me to match to my work, I did find some of it that made sense and took note to pay attention to those areas in the next book I wrote. Honestly, it was only this year (2020) that I stopped feeding all my characters pasta at meals.

I like fettuccine Alfredo, okay! If you didn't see that as a Cara North tell before, if you read my books you will identify it now. You will have this tell. I am an avid fan of an author that once I noticed my meal habit, I was able to see hers. She feeds at least one character in each book a grilled cheese sandwich. I looked. It made me instantly realize this is just what we do, and she probably doesn't realize it, or maybe she does it intentionally. South Park writers Trey Parker and Matt Stone killed character, Kenny in every episode because it was an ongoing theme that people began to expect and anticipate. It doesn't have to work against you if you are aware you are doing it.

If you only have one book and it is a standalone without connection to any others, you can still learn from reviews. If it is a series, WAIT! After the series is complete, I combed through the reviews looking for both good and bad comments so I could decide what is valid and what is just snark or a book someone didn't like. Once I can identify some valid points in criticism, then I can work on that in future writing.

Some things to remember:
- Every book gets a bad review at some point
- No review should impact your motivation to write
- If you have a series, wait to read reviews or at least have a plan to self-care if you see a bad one
- Good reviews can be just at paralyzing as bad ones so have a plan in place for that also
- Try to uncover your own quirks (pasta anyone?) and diversify.

What is your Self Support strategy for dealing with reviews?

    If you have not released your book yet, take some time to think about this and put a plan in place. Part of that plan may be connecting with someone you identify as a supporter of your work. Part of it may be to ignore until you are ready. Part of it may be to kill them...in your next book of course.

Self Support Plan for Reviews:

Learning Opportunities

I know you are thinking that what I am about to say is just because I offer lessons and I am an educator. The second part is true. If you want to continue learning from me, that is great. Still, if you chose to read other how-to books or find other learning platforms, and I actually suggest that you do to get a variety if ideas, I still want you to look for ways to continue your professional development. The truth is if you are writing for publication, you are becoming or enhancing your skills in a profession.

The profession of writing like all other work requires you to be current and knowledgeable of your craft. Take advantage of every free class, every reasonably priced lesson you can take. The more you learn, the better you will become. Do not stop seeking new ways to explore your craft. If you write fiction, look at some non-fiction courses and books and vice versa.

Do not let the learning stop the writing but do build it into your schedule to read a book or take a class about an element within this industry at least once a month.

If you want to continue this endeavor with me, you can find more information at:

www.creativewritingwithdrnagle.com

Notes

About the Author

Tonya Nagle is a writer, educator, podcaster, coach, veteran, and so many more titles. Essentially, I am living my life and doing the best I can, just like you. It is not always easy so I appreciate the times that run smoothly so I can endure the times that are a bit unpredictable.

I hope you will be on the lookout for the next resource!

www.ingramcontent.com/pod-product-compliance
Lightning Source LLC
Chambersburg PA
CBHW022109170526
45157CB00004B/1549